debbie
macomber

Dear Friends,

Have you ever thought about what it would take to make yourself really happy, or at least to feel more alive?

You might be surprised what a life-changing influence it can be...not only to just think about it, but also to make an actual list of, say 20, dreams and goals. In my latest novel, *Twenty Wishes*, four widows stumble upon the idea while trying to help one another endure Valentine's Day without someone to love.

The excerpts in this companion knitting book tell you a little about what happens next in their lives. If you've read my earlier Blossom Street novels, of course, you know knitting *has* to be involved if someone is trying to find happiness! I am thrilled with the knit designs that my friends at Leisure Arts developed to tie in with the story, from a beginner's scarf to pretty sweaters and cozy wraps.

As a knit-o-holic myself, I'm also pleased with the designer line of knitting organizers and accessories that Leisure Arts and I have collaborated on. This new Knit Along with Debbie Macomber collection offers beautiful totes and storage options, a purse kit, classic patterns, and handy knitting notions. I'm wild about the soft and timeless color palette, too! One of my favorite items is The Knitter's Complete Journal. Imagine—all of your knitting notes in one place, plus a CD full of printable note cards, tags, and more! You can see the full line at *TheLeisureBoutique.com* or at your favorite knitting shop.

Something else that you and I both can feel good about is that I've donated all the proceeds from sales of my Leisure Arts Knit Along books and new product line to my favorite charities: Warm Up America!, Project Linus, Guideposts Knit for Kids, and World Vision. There's even an afghan block pattern on page 41 to help you get started with your own community charity efforts.

My greatest hope is that my publications and products will help you discover the rich rewards of knitting for yourself and those you love. I look forward to hearing from you!

Debbie

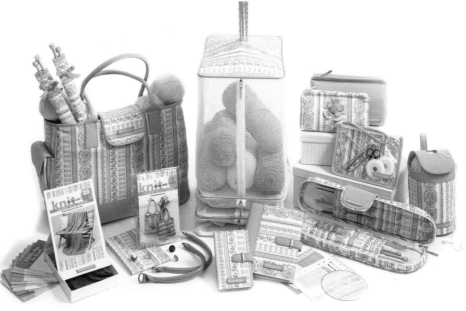

LEISURE ARTS, INC.
Little Rock, Arkansas

a word from LEISURE ARTS and MIRA books

Read The Books that Inspired the Projects

Through the novels in her Blossom Street series, Debbie Macomber has introduced us to many fascinating women who share their joys and heartaches through friendships forged by their love of knitting. To help you experience the rewards of knitting just like Debbie's characters, Leisure Arts is excited to offer this latest companion publication to the popular book series. *Knit Along with Debbie Macomber—Twenty Wishes* is filled with 15 knit designs inspired by the story.

You'll enjoy excerpts from Debbie's book as you decide which to knit first: a scarf, felted book carrier, lap robe, spa set, beaded garter, dog coat, afghan, baby bonnet and mittens, girl's sweater, scarf and beret set, doily, and woman's sweater. Also included is a pattern for an afghan block that you can make to contribute to one of Debbie's favorite nonprofit organizations, *Warm Up America!*

For more knitting fun with Debbie, look for these Leisure Arts instruction books in the *Knit Along with Debbie Macomber* collection: *The Shop on Blossom Street, A Good Yarn, Back on Blossom Street, The Cedar Cove Collection,* and *Debbie's Favorites.*

Read all of Debbie's heartwarming stories, then knit up a little creativity from Leisure Arts.

Leaflet# 4279

Leaflet# 4135

Leaflet# 4132

LOOK FOR DEBBIE'S HEARTWARMING STORIES AT BOOKSTORES EVERYWHERE, AND COLLECT ALL THE KNITTING PUBLICATIONS INSPIRED BY HER BLOSSOM STREET NOVELS.

To find out more about Debbie Macomber, visit www.debbiemacomber.com or www.mirabooks.com.

Visit **www.leisurearts.com** to sign up for our Free E-Newsletter and shop online at **www.theleisureboutique.com**.

Everything for pets....**www.freepetprojects.com**

Anne Marie Roche

It was six o'clock on Valentine's Day, an hour that should have marked the beginning of a celebration—the way it used to when she and Robert were married. When Robert was alive. But tonight, on the most romantic day of the year, thirty-eight-year-old Anne Marie Roche was alone. Turning over the Closed sign on the door of Blossom Street Books, she glanced at the Valentine's display with its romance novels she didn't read anymore. The truth was, Anne Marie hated her life. Well, okay, hate was putting it too strongly. After all, she was healthy, reasonably young and attractive, financially solvent, and she owned the most popular bookstore in the area. But she didn't have anyone to love, anyone who loved her. Her husband had died nine months ago. They'd been happy together, well-matched in every way but one. Anne Marie had wanted a baby. Robert didn't. He'd had a family—two children—with his first wife and wasn't interested in starting a second one. His solution had been to buy her a dog. She'd still wanted a baby.

After learning that Valentine's Day was perhaps the most difficult holiday for widows, Anne Marie and her friends had decided to plan their own celebration. Only instead of romantic love and marriage, they'd celebrate friendship and defy the rest of the world's pitying glances. So tonight she had closed the store early and set up the back room with champagne, chocolate, and lots of bubble wrap to pop. The noise had added an unexpected sense of fun and exhilaration as they discussed how to revive their enthusiasm for life with a list of twenty wishes.

Lillie Higgins and Barbie Foster

*L*illie and Barbie were a unique pair of widows; mother and daughter. They'd lost their husbands in a private plane crash three years earlier. Anne Marie remembered reading about the Learjet incident in the paper; both pilots and their two passengers had been killed in a freak accident on landing. Lillie's husband and his son-in-law were executives in a perfume company and often took business trips together.

Lillie Higgins was close to Elise's age, but that was all they shared. Actually, it was difficult to tell exactly how old Lillie was. She looked barely fifty, but with a forty-year-old daughter, she had to be in her mid-sixties. Petite and delicate, she was one of those rare women who never seemed to age. Lillie's wardrobe consisted of ultra-expensive knits and gold jewelry, and Anne Marie had the impression that if she wanted, she could purchase this bookstore ten times over.

Her daughter, Barbie Foster, was very much like her and aptly named, at least as far as appearances went. She had long blond hair that never seemed to get mussed, gorgeous crystal-blue eyes, a flawless figure. It was hard to believe she had eighteen-year-old twin sons who were college freshmen; Anne Marie would bet she looked more like their sister than their mother. If Anne Marie didn't like Barbie so much, it would be easy to resent her for being…so perfect.

Elise Beaumont

Anne Marie opened the door as Elise Beaumont approached. Elise's husband, Maverick, had recently passed away after a long battle with cancer. In her mid-sixties, she was a retired librarian who'd reconnected with her divorced husband after nearly thirty years, only to lose him again after less than three. She was a slight, gray-haired woman who'd become almost gaunt. The veil of fresh grief hung over her, but the sternness of her features was softened by the sadness in her eyes. A frequent patron of the bookstore, she and Anne Marie had become friends during the months of Maverick's decline. In many ways his death was a release, yet Anne Marie understood how difficult it was to let go of someone you loved.

Last week when Anne Marie had spoken to Elise, she'd decided to apply for a part-time job. For the three years of her husband's illness, Elise had been Maverick's primary caregiver. Now that her husband was gone, she had time on her hands—time she needed to fill.

Ellen Falk

After the Lunch Buddy orientation meeting, Helen Mayer handed out the assignments and left Anne Marie for last. "The child I have in mind for you is named Ellen Falk," the school counselor eventually said. "Ellen is eight years old and in second grade. Because of the Right to Privacy Laws, I'm not allowed to reveal any details about her home background. However, I can tell you that Ellen is currently living with her maternal grandmother. Ellen is an intense child. Very quiet. Shy. She doesn't have a lot to say, but don't let that discourage you. Talk to her and be patient. She'll speak to you when she's ready."

Oh, great. Anne Marie would have to carry the entire conversation for heaven only knew how many weeks. "Is there a reason you decided to match me up with this child?" she asked. Anne Marie wasn't much of a talker herself these days, and she wasn't sure that pairing her with an intense, reticent child would work.

"Ellen loves to read," Helen said. "And since you own Blossom Street Books...well, it seemed to be a good fit."

seed stitch scarf

Ellen had hoped her grandmother would teach her to knit someday, but now Grandma Dolores was in the hospital recovering from heart surgery. When Anne Marie suggested they learn together, Ellen decided her first project should be something to cheer up her dear relative.

● □ □ □ **BEGINNER**

Finished Size: 3" x 72" (7.5 cm x 183 cm)

MATERIALS

Bulky Weight Variegated Yarn
[2.8 ounces, 134 yards
(80 grams, 123 meters) per skein]:
  2 skeins
Straight knitting needles, size 10 (6 mm)
  or size needed for gauge
Yarn needle

GAUGE: In Seed Stitch, 11 sts = 3" (7.5 cm)

SCARF

Cast on 11 sts.

Row 1: K1, (P1, K1) across.

Repeat Row 1 for Seed Stitch until Scarf measures approximately 72" (183 cm) from cast on edge **or** to desired length.

Bind off all stitches in pattern.

Weave in yarn ends.

"I want to knit something for my Grandma Dolores," Ellen stated. "Something pretty...for her to wear to church."

"What about a scarf?" Anne Marie suggested. She'd seen several that were exquisite. Elise had explained that these elaborate scarves had been knit using the basic stitch she'd taught Anne Marie that very day.

—Anne Marie

felted book carrier

Now that Anne Marie had learned to knit and purl, she looked forward to taking Elise's class on felting. Still, it amazed her that the two basic stitches were all she needed to create a beautiful bag like this one.

■□□□ BEGINNER

Finished Size: 13" x 14" (33 cm x 35.5 cm)
Before Felting: 20" x 30" (51 cm x 76 cm)

MATERIALS

Medium Weight Variegated Wool Yarn [2.8 ounces, 110 yards (80 grams, 101 meters) per skein]:
   6 skeins
Note: The yarn you choose is what makes the Carrier interesting. We used yarn with a 70% wool content. The higher the wool content, the better. Avoid wool yarn that has been super washed, it will not felt.
   Straight knitting needles, size 11 (8 mm)
      or size needed for gauge
   Yarn needle
   Upholstery thread
   3/4" (19 mm) Buttons - 4

GAUGE: In Stockinette Stitch,
         12 sts and 15 rows = 4" (10 cm)

BODY (Make 2)

Cast on 60 sts.

Work in Stockinette Stitch (knit one row, purl one row) until Body measures approximately 30" (76 cm) from cast on edge.

Bind off all stitches leaving a long end for sewing on one piece.

With **right** sides together, sew Body across both sides and cast on edge; turn right side out.

STRAP (Make 2)

Cast on 9 sts.

Work in Stockinette Stitch until Strap measures approximately 52" (132 cm) from cast on edge.

Bind off all stitches.

FELTING

To keep the opening from flaring, it helps to run a cotton thread around the opening and again 1/2" (1.5 cm) below, gathering slightly. Pull the threads out while the item is still wet.

Machine Felting

Use ONLY a top-loading washer. Use the HOT wash setting with a COLD rinse cycle at the lowest water level setting. DO NOT LET IT SPIN. This can cause creases that don't come out. Our model was felted using 1 tablespoon of detergent.

Place your Book Carrier (Body and Straps) in a tight-mesh sweater bag to contain the fuzz your Carrier may shed. Check your Carrier every 2-3 minutes to monitor for size and shrinkage. When you check your Carrier, wear rubber gloves to protect your hands. Be careful, the water is very hot. If your Carrier is not felted enough by the end of the wash cycle, repeat as needed and continue to check your Carrier frequently. If your Carrier is left in the hot water too long, it can become too small and the fabric too tight.

We do NOT recommend putting felted projects in the dryer. They will continue to shrink and shed and change their shape.

Anne Marie and Elise had met Lillie and Barbie in a book group at the store. After Robert died, Elise had suggested reading Lolly Winston's *Good Grief*, a novel about a young woman adjusting to widowhood. Although the larger group had read and discussed other books, the four widows had gravitated together and begun to meet on their own.

—*Anne Marie*

Blocking

Remove your Carrier from the sweater bag and roll it in a towel and gently squeeze out the excess water. DO NOT WRING.

Block IMMEDIATELY. Form it into the size and shape you want by pulling and patting. Place a plastic grocery bag inside out over cardboard cut to desired size. This is used to make it easier to pull the felted Carrier over the board. Place the Carrier over the end of the cardboard and pull downward until the entire Carrier is on the board. Pin Straps to a board.

Let your Carrier air dry even though it may take several days.

Using upholstery thread and placing a button on each end of each Strap, sew each Strap to right side of Body, 1½" (4 cm) from seam.

two-tone throw

Knitting a lap robe for Ellen's grandmother would count toward Anne Marie's goal of practicing not-so-random acts of kindness. Although she knew the simple, classic pattern would look good in any color, she chose a soft lavender for Dolores' gift.

◐■□□ **EASY**

Finished Size: 32¹/₂" x 48" (82.5 cm x 122 cm)

MATERIALS
Bulky Weight Yarn
[3.5 ounces, 148 yards
(100 grams, 136 meters) per skein]:
  Taupe - 5 skeins
  Black - 4 skeins
29" (73.5 cm) Circular knitting needle,
  size 10¹/₂ (6.5 mm) **or** size needed for gauge

GAUGE: In pattern, 14 sts = 3³/₄" (9.5 cm)
and 24 rows = 3¹/₂" (9 cm)

BODY

With Taupe cast on 121 sts.

Rows 1 and 2: With Taupe, knit across.

Note: When instructed to slip a stitch, always slip as if to **purl** with yarn held on the **wrong** side.

Row 3 (Right side): With Black, K3, slip 1, (K1, slip 1) across to last 3 sts, K3.

Row 4: K3, with yarn forward slip 1, (K1, with yarn forward slip 1) across to last 3 sts, K3.

Repeat Rows 1-4 for pattern until piece measures approximately 48" (122 cm) from cast on edge, ending by working Row 2.

Bind off all sts in **knit**.

W asn't that what Elise had said? Doing something for someone else made you feel better about yourself.

—Barbie

Anne Marie was looking forward to sitting down in front of the TV with her new project. She'd gone to A Good Yarn on her lunch break to buy the necessary knitting supplies. Elise had helped Anne Marie select her yarn and needles. The choices seemed endless, and after much debate, she'd selected a soft washable wool in lavender to make a lap robe for Dolores Falk.

—Anne Marie

refreshing spa set

Although in her mid-sixties, Lillie Higgins looked barely fifty. Her favorite ocean resort was a place she could find solace and pamper herself with baths and facials using plush comforts such as this spa set.

■■□□ **EASY**

Finished Sizes
  Headband: 3¹/₂" wide x 18¹/₂" circumference (9 cm x 47 cm)
  Face Cloth: 8¹/₂" x 9" (21.5 cm x 23 cm)

MATERIALS
  Medium Weight Cotton Yarn
  [3.5 ounces, 207 yards
  (100 grams, 188 meters) per skein]:
    1 skein (for set)
  Straight knitting needles, size 8 (5 mm)
    or size needed for gauge
  Yarn needle

GAUGE: In pattern, 15 sts (3 repeats) and 17 rows = 3¹/₂" (9 cm) relaxed

HEADBAND
Cast on 82 sts.

Row 1 (Right side)**:** P2, (K3, P2) across.

Row 2: K2, (P3, K2) across.

Row 3: P2, ★ K2 tog (*Fig. 11, page 44*), YO (*Fig. 6a, page 43*), K1, P2; repeat from ★ across.

Row 4: K2, (P3, K2) across.

Row 5: P2, (K3, P2) across.

Row 6: K2, (P3, K2) across.

Row 7: P2, ★ K1, YO, [slip 1 as if to **knit**, K1, PSSO (*Figs. 13a & b, page 45*)], P2; repeat from ★ across.

Row 8: K2, (P3, K2) across.

Rows 9-17: Repeat Rows 1-8 once, then repeat Row 1 once **more**.

Bind off all sts in pattern, leaving a long end for sewing.

Weave end of rows together (*Fig. 21, page 46*).

FACE CLOTH
Cast on 38 sts.

Rows 1-4: Knit across.

Row 5 (Right side)**:** K3, (P2, K3) across.

Row 6: K5, P3, (K2, P3) across to last 5 sts, K5.

Row 7: K3, P2, ★ K2 tog (*Fig. 11, page 44*), YO (*Fig. 6a, page 43*), K1, P2; repeat from ★ across to last 3 sts, K3.

Row 8: K5, P3, (K2, P3) across to last 5 sts, K5.

Row 9: K3, (P2, K3) across.

Row 10: K5, P3, (K2, P3) across to last 5 sts, K5.

Lillie Higgins paid extra-close attention to her makeup Friday morning, chastising herself the entire time. Anyone who even suspected she was preening and primping for the service department manager at a car dealership would be aghast.

—*Lillie*

Row 11: K3, P2, ★ K1, YO, [slip 1 as if to **knit**, K1, PSSO *(Figs. 13a & b, page 45)*], P2; repeat from ★ across to last 3 sts, K3.

Row 12: K5, P3, (K2, P3) across to last 5 sts, K5.

Rows 13-45: Repeat Rows 5-12, 4 times; then repeat Row 5 once **more**.

Rows 46-49: Knit across.

Bind off all sts in **knit**.

beaded garter

As the small chapel reverberated with the traditional wedding march, Anne Marie felt her heart swell with joy as Melissa walked past her. The lacy garter that Anne Marie had knit was only one tiny part of all the things she had done to help her stepdaughter prepare for this day.

◀■■☐☐ **EASY**

Finished Size: 1" (2.5 cm) wide x desired length

MATERIALS
Cotton Thread size 5
[100 yards (91 meters) per ball]:
  1 ball
Straight knitting needles, size 3 (3.25 mm)
  or size needed for gauge
Tapestry needle (small enough to go
  through bead and large enough for thread
  to go into eye)
6/0 Seed beads
¹/₈" (3 mm) wide Satin ribbon - 1 yard

GAUGE: In pattern,
  12 rows (2 scallops) = 1¹/₂" (3.75 cm)

GARTER
You'll need 8 beads for every 3" (3.75 cm). Decide how long you want your Garter to be, then divide that length by 3 and multiply the answer by 8.
Example: For a 21" (53.5 cm) Garter, you'll need 56 beads (21" divided by 3" = 7 x 8 beads = 56).

Thread tapestry needle with crochet thread and string required number of beads onto crochet thread, adding extra beads just to make sure you have enough.

Cast on 6 sts.

Tip: Work edge sts firmly to prevent loopy sts.

Row 1: Knit across.

Row 2 (Right side)**:** K2, K2 tog *(Fig. 11, page 44)*, YO *(Fig. 6a, page 43)*, K2.

Row 3: Knit across.

Row 4: K2, slip bead up, YO twice, K2 tog, YO, K2: 8 sts.

Row 5: K4, drop next YO forming a large loop and (K1, P1) twice **all** in loop leaving loop on left needle, slip bead on loop next to right needle and (K1, P1) twice **all** in same loop, K2: 14 sts.

Tip: When binding off sts, keep bound off (formed) sts small.

Row 6: Bind off 8 sts, K1, K2 tog, YO, K2: 6 sts.

These lists of Twenty Wishes seemed to be influencing all their lives—and those of others, too, Anne Marie noticed. For instance, Elise's wish had been a solution to Lydia's problem of teaching too many classes. Now Elise would fill in as sales help when necessary and teach three classes. In addition to the beginner's class, she'd be teaching a class on knitting with beads and another on felted purses.

—Anne Marie

Row 7: K1, slip bead up, knit across pushing bead to back (right side).

Row 8: K2, K2 tog, YO, K2.

Repeat Rows 3-8 for pattern until Garter measures desired length, ending by working Row 3.

Bind off all sts in **knit** leaving a long end for sewing.

Sew ends together.

Wash and block Edging *(see Washing and Blocking, page 47)*.

Beginning at center, weave ribbon through spaces; tie in a bow.

Design by Cathy Hardy.

baxter's cozy coat

Anne Marie's ever-faithful Baxter shared her tiny apartment above the bookstore. No matter the weather, their morning routine never varied: with the coffee brewing, she took the little Yorkie down Blossom Street for two blocks, going around a small park twice and then back.

⬤◼☐☐ **EASY**

Size	Chest Measurement
X-Small	12" (30.5 cm)
Small	16" (40.5 cm)
Medium	20" (51 cm)
Large	24" (61 cm)
X-Large	28" (71 cm)
XX-Large	32" (81.5 cm)

Note: Instructions are written for sizes X-Small, Small, and Medium in the first set of braces { }, with sizes Large, X-Large and XX-Large in the second set of braces. Instructions will be easier to read if you circle all the numbers pertaining to your dog's size. If only one number is given, it applies to all sizes.

MATERIALS

Medium Weight Yarn
[3.5 ounces, 170 yards
(100 grams, 156 meters) per skein]:
　{1-1-2}{2-2-3} skein(s)
Straight knitting needles, sizes 7 (4.5 mm)
　and 9 (5.5 mm) **or** sizes needed for gauge
Yarn needle
³/₄" (19 mm) Buttons - {1-1-1}{2-2-2}

GAUGE: With larger size needles, in pattern,
　　16 sts and 26 rows = 4" (10 cm)

BODY

With larger size needles,
cast on {27-37-47}{57-67-77} sts.

Rows 1-5: Knit across.

Row 6: K5, ★ P2 tog without slipping sts off needle (*Fig. 17, page 45*), then knit same 2 sts together (*Fig. 11, page 44*); repeat from ★ across to last 4 sts, K4.

Row 7 (Right side): Knit across.

Row 8: K4, ★ P2 tog without slipping sts off needle, then knit same 2 sts together; repeat from ★ across to last 5 sts, K5.

Row 9: Knit across.

Repeat Rows 6-9 for pattern until Body measures approximately {6¹/₄-8³/₄-11¹/₂} {13¹/₂-15¹/₂-17¹/₂}"/{16-22-29}{34.5-39.5-44.5} cm from cast on edge **or** to within {1¹/₄-1¹/₄-1¹/₂}{1¹/₂-1¹/₂-1¹/₂}"/{3-3-4}{4-4-4} cm of desired length to base of neck.

NECK SHAPING

Continue working in pattern, increasing one stitch at each edge (*Figs. 9a & b, page 44*), every other row, {4-4-5}{5-5-5} times, knitting new stitches: {35-45-57}{67-77-87} sts.

Anne Marie set her bags on the kitchen table, then scooped up her dog, stroking his silky fur. "Hey, Mr. Baxter." He wriggled excitedly and she put him down, collecting a biscuit from a box on the counter. "Here you go." She smiled as he loudly crunched his cookie, licking up each and every crumb. "Maybe I'll knit you a little coat sometime."

—Anne Marie

NECK RIBBING
Change to smaller size needles.

Work in K1, P1 ribbing for {3-4-4}{5-5-6}"/ {7.5-10-10}{12.5-12.5-15} cm.

Bind off all sts **loosely** in ribbing.

BAND
With smaller size needles, cast on {7-9-11}{15-17-19} sts.

Knit 4 rows.

SIZES X-SMALL, SMALL AND MEDIUM ONLY
Buttonhole Row: K{2-3-4}, K2 tog, YO *(Fig. 6a, page 43)*, knit across.

Instructions continued on page 23.

pretty panels afghan

Anne Marie had purposely kept her furniture in storage to avoid dealing with the past. Her fear was that the household goods she'd shared with Robert would trigger too many memories. But now she was looking forward to decorating her new home with cozy comforts.

■■□□ EASY

Finished Size: 46¹/₂" x 66" (118 cm x 167.5 cm)

MATERIALS
   Bulky Weight Yarn
   [3 ounces, 135 yards
   (85 grams, 123 meters) per skein]:
      Rose - 7 skeins
      Brown - 4 skeins
   Straight knitting needles, size 11 (8 mm)
      or size needed for gauge
   Cable needle
   Yarn needle

GAUGE: In Stockinette Stitch,
          11 sts and 16 rows = 4" (10 cm)

LACE PANEL (Make 3)
Finished Width: 10¹/₂" (26.5 cm)

With Rose, cast on 29 sts.

Row 1 (Right side)**:** K1, (P1, K1) across.

Note: Always slip the first stitch as if to **purl** with yarn forward.

Rows 2-4: Slip 1, (P1, K1) across.

Row 5: Slip 1, P1, K 25, P1, K1.

Row 6 AND ALL WRONG SIDE ROWS: Slip 1, P1, K1, P 23, K1, P1, K1.

Row 7: Slip 1, P1, K 25, P1, K1.

Row 9: Slip 1, P1, K 10, K2 tog (*Fig. 11, page 44*), YO (*Fig. 6a, page 43*), K1, YO, [slip 1 as if to **knit**, K1, PSSO (*Figs. 13a & b, page 45*)], K 10, P1, K1.

Row 11: Slip 1, P1, K9, K2 tog, YO, K3, YO, slip 1 as if to **knit**, K1, PSSO, K9, P1, K1.

Row 13: Slip 1, P1, K8, (K2 tog, YO) twice, K1, (YO, slip 1 as if to **knit**, K1, PSSO) twice, K8, P1, K1.

Row 15: Slip 1, P1, K7, (K2 tog, YO) twice, K3, (YO, slip 1 as if to **knit**, K1, PSSO) twice, K7, P1, K1.

Row 17: Slip 1, P1, K6, (K2 tog, YO) 3 times, K1, (YO, slip 1 as if to **knit**, K1, PSSO) 3 times, K6, P1, K1.

Rows 18-260: Repeat Rows 6-17, 20 times; then repeat Rows 6-8 once **more**.

Rows 261-264: Slip 1, (P1, K1) across.

Bind off all sts in pattern.

After school on Tuesday, Anne Marie had taken Ellen to A Good Yarn and allowed her to purchase yarn and needles of her own. That evening, after the dinner dishes and Ellen's homework, they'd sat knitting side by side, helping each other. Anne Marie couldn't avoid reflecting that this was something she'd never had the chance to do with her stepdaughter.

—Anne Marie

CABLE PANEL (Make 2)
Finished Width: 7¹/₂" (19 cm)

With Brown, cast on 22 sts.

Row 1 (Right side): (K1, P1) across.

Note: Always slip the first stitch as if to **purl** with yarn forward.

Row 2: Slip 1, K1, (P1, K1) across.

Row 3: Slip 1, P1, (K1, P1) across to last 2 sts, K2.

Row 4: Slip 1, K1, (P1, K1) across.

Row 5: Slip 1, P2, K2, P3, K2, (M1, K2) twice *(Figs. 10a & b, page 44)*, P3, K2, P1, K2: 24 sts.

Row 6: Slip 1, K2, P2, K3, P8, K3, P2, K1, P1, K1.

Instructions continued on page 23.

bobbles for baby

Realizing that family could come about in the most unexpected ways, Anne Marie vowed to be a wonderful grandmother for her stepdaughter's baby. Of course, that would involve knitting all kinds of precious things like bonnets and mittens and more!

■■■□ INTERMEDIATE

Size: Newborn

MATERIALS

Medium Weight Yarn
[5 ounces, 256 yards
(140 grams, 234 meters) per skein]:
  1 skein
Straight knitting needles, sizes 5 (3.75 mm)
  and 7 (4.5 mm) **or** sizes needed for gauge
Yarn needle
1/2" (12 mm) Button - 1

GAUGE: With larger size needles,
in Stockinette Stitch,
20 sts and 28 rows = 4" (10 cm)

PATTERN STITCHES

MOSS STITCH *(6 sts)*
Rows 1 and 2: (K1, P1) 3 times.
Rows 3 and 4: (P1, K1) 3 times.
Repeat Rows 1-4 for pattern.

EYELET RIBS & BOBBLES *(20 sts)*
Row 1: P2, K3, P2, K6, P2, K3, P2.
Row 2: K2, P3, K2, P6, K2, P3, K2.
Row 3: P2, [with yarn in back slip 1 as if to **purl**, K2, PSSO *(Fig. 14, page 45)*], P2, K6, P2, with yarn in back slip 1 as if to **purl**, K2, PSSO, P2: 18 sts.
Row 4: K2, P1, YO *(Fig. 6b, page 44)*, P1, K2, P6, K2, P1, YO, P1, K2: 20 sts.

Rows 5-8: Repeat Rows 1-4.
Row 9: P2, K3, P2, K2, (K, K tbl, K, K tbl) **all** in the next st, K1, **turn**; P4, **turn**; K4, **turn**; P4, **turn**; slip the second, third, and fourth st on the left needle over the first st on the left needle **(Bobble made)**, K tbl of Bobble, K2, P2, K3, P2.
Repeat Rows 2-9 for pattern.

MOSS DIAMOND *(21 sts)*
Row 1: P1, (K1, P1) 3 times, K7, P1, (K1, P1) 3 times.
Row 2: K1, (P1, K1) 3 times, P7, K1, (P1, K1) 3 times.
Row 3: (K1, P1) 3 times, K4, P1, K4, (P1, K1) 3 times.
Row 4: (P1, K1) 3 times, P4, K1, P4, (K1, P1) 3 times.
Row 5: K2, P1, K1, P1, (K4, P1, K1, P1) twice, K2.
Row 6: P2, K1, P1, K1, (P4, K1, P1, K1) twice, P2.
Row 7: K3, P1, K4, P1, (K1, P1) twice, K4, P1, K3.
Row 8: P3, K1, P4, K1, (P1, K1) twice, P4, K1, P3.
Row 9: K7, P1, (K1, P1) 3 times, K7.
Row 10: P7, K1, (P1, K1) 3 times, P7.
Rows 11-16: Repeat Rows 7 and 8, then repeat Rows 5 and 6, then repeat Rows 3 and 4.
Repeat Rows 1-16 for pattern.

BONNET
TWISTED RIBBING

With smaller size needles, cast on 73 sts.

Row 1: P1, (K1 tbl, P1) across *(Fig. 8, page 44)*.

Row 2: K1 tbl, (P1, K1 tbl) across.

Repeat Rows 1 and 2 until ribbing measures approximately 1" (2.5 cm), ending by working Row 1.

BODY

Change to larger size needles.

Row 1 (Right side)**:** Work Row 1 of Moss Stitch, work Row 1 of Eyelet Ribs & Bobbles, work Row 1 of Moss Diamond, work Row 1 of Eyelet Ribs & Bobbles, work Row 1 of Moss Stitch.

Instructions continued on page 22.

Rows 2-32: Work next row of Moss Stitch, work next row of Eyelet Ribs & Bobbles, work next row of Moss Diamond, work next row of Eyelet Ribs & Bobbles, work next row of Moss Stitch.

Maintain established pattern throughout.

Rows 33 and 34: Bind off 6 sts, work across: 61 sts.

Row 35: Bind off 7 sts, work across to last 7 sts, P2, K3, P2: 54 sts.

Row 36: Bind off 7 sts, work across: 47 sts.

Rows 37-40: Repeat Rows 33-36: 21 sts.

Bind off all sts **loosely** in pattern.

CHIN STRAP
With smaller size needles, cast on 20 sts.

Rows 1 and 2: (K1 tbl, P1) across.

Row 3 (Buttonhole row): K1 tbl, P1, slip 1 tbl as if to **purl**, K1, PSSO, YO *(Fig. 6a, page 43)*, (K1 tbl, P1) across.

Rows 4 and 5: (K1 tbl, P1) across.

Bind off all sts **loosely** in pattern.

FINISHING
Make a short twisted cord *(see Twisted Cord, page 46)* and attach a 3" (7.5 cm) tassel to one end *(Figs. 22a & b, page 47)*.

Fold Bonnet in half and sew bound off edge together for back seam, inserting twisted cord at peak.

Fold Ribbing to right side and tack in place. Sew button to one side of Bonnet and Chin Strap to the other.

MITTENS
TWISTED RIBBING
With smaller size needles, cast on 29 sts.

Row 1: P1, (K1 tbl, P1) across *(Fig. 8, page 44)*.

Row 2: K1 tbl, (P1, K1 tbl) across.

Repeat Rows 1 and 2 until ribbing measures approximately 2" (5 cm), ending by working Row 2.

Eyelet Row: (K2 tog tbl, YO) across to last st *(Fig. 12, page 45 and Fig. 6a, page 43)*, K1.

BODY
Change to larger size needles.

Row 1: P6, purl into the **front** and into the **back** of the next st, P 15, purl into the **front** and into the **back** of the next st, P6: 31 sts.

Row 2 (Right side): K1, (P1, K1) 5 times, P3, K3, P2, (K1, P1) 6 times.

Row 3: (K1, P1) 6 times, K2, P3, K3, P1, (K1, P1) 5 times.

Row 4: (P1, K1) 6 times, P2, [with yarn in back slip 1 as if to **purl**, K2, PSSO *(Fig. 14, page 45)*], P3, K1, (P1, K1) 5 times: 30 sts.

Row 5: P1, (K1, P1) 5 times, K3, P1, YO *(Fig. 6b, page 44)*, P1, K2, (P1, K1) 6 times: 31 sts.

Rows 6-23: Repeat Rows 2-5, 4 times; then repeat Rows 2 and 3 once **more**.

Row 24: K2 tog 6 times *(Fig. 11, page 44)*, P2 tog *(Fig. 17, page 45)*, [with yarn in back slip 1 as if to **purl**, K2 tog, PSSO *(Fig. 15, page 45)*], P2 tog, K2 tog 6 times; cut yarn leaving a long end for sewing: 15 sts.

FINISHING

Thread needle with long end and slip through remaining 15 sts; gather tightly and secure. Weave back seam *(Fig. 21, page 46)*.

Make two 14" (35.5 cm) twisted cords *(see Twisted Cord, page 46)*; lace one through Eyelet row of each Mitten.

Make a 32" (81.5 cm) twisted cord; sew one end of cord inside each Mitten at center top of Ribbing.

Design by Beth MacDonald.

baxter's cozy coat
continued from page 17.

SIZES LARGE, X-LARGE AND XX-LARGE ONLY
Buttonhole Row: K2, K2 tog, YO *(Fig. 6a, page 43)*, K{6-8-10}, K2 tog, YO, K3.

Knit every row until Band measures approximately {5-6$\frac{1}{2}$-8}{9$\frac{1}{2}$-11-12$\frac{1}{2}$}"/ {12.5-16.5-20.5}{24-28-32} cm from cast on edge **or** to desired length.

Bind off all sts leaving a long end for sewing.

FINISHING
Place the Coat on your dog and mark placement for Band. Sew Band in place.

Sew button(s) to Coat to correspond with buttonhole(s).

Beginning at end of Neck Shaping, sew end of rows on Neck Ribbing together to halfway point; fold Collar to right side.

Design by Cathy Hardy.

pretty panels afghan
continued from page 19.

Row 7: Slip 1, P2, K2, P3, K8, P3, K2, P1, K2.

Row 8: Slip 1, K2, P2, K3, P8, K3, P2, K1, P1, K1.

To work Cable (uses 8 sts), slip next 4 stitches onto cable needle and hold in **front** of work, K4 from left needle, K4 from cable needle.

Row 9: Slip 1, P2, K2, P3, work Cable, P3, K2, P1, K2.

Row 10: Slip 1, K2, P2, K3, P8, K3, P2, K1, P1, K1.

Rows 11-16: Repeat Rows 7 and 8, 3 times.

Rows 17-260: Repeat Rows 9-16, 30 times; then repeat Rows 9-12 once **more**.

Row 261: Slip 1, P2, K2, P3, K2, K2 tog twice, K2, P3, K2, P1, K2: 22 sts.

Row 262: Slip 1, K1, (P1, K1) across.

Row 263: Slip 1, P1, (K1, P1) across to last 2 sts, K2.

Rows 264 and 265: Repeat Rows 262 and 263.

Bind off all sts in pattern.

ASSEMBLY
Whipstitch Panels together *(Fig. 20, page 46)*, placing cast on edge of each Panel at the same end and alternating Lace and Cable Panels.

Design by Cathy Hardy.

raglan ridge pullover

*When Anne Marie began assembling her Twenty Wishes scrapbook,
a hand-knit sweater was one of the first few pictures she cut out.
That represented Wish No. 2: Learn to knit. Pasting it in place, she thought
about needing a photo of Ellen, too—maybe in a sweater she'd knit.*

■■■□ INTERMEDIATE

Size	Finished Chest Measurement	
4	24½"	(62 cm)
6	26¼"	(66.5 cm)
8	28¼"	(72 cm)
10	30"	(76 cm)
12	32"	(81.5 cm)

Note: Instructions are written for sizes 4 and 6 in the first set of braces { }, with sizes 8,10 and 12 in the second set of braces. Instructions will be easier to read if you circle all the numbers pertaining to your child's size. If only one number is given, it applies to all sizes.

MATERIALS

Medium Weight Cotton Yarn
[3.5 ounces, 207 yards
(100 grams, 188 meters) per skein]:
   {2-3}{3-3-4} skeins
Straight knitting needles, sizes 6 (4 mm)
   and 8 (5 mm) **or** sizes needed for gauge
16" (40.5 cm), 24" (61 cm) and 29"
   (73.5 cm) Circular knitting needles,
   sizes 6 (4 mm) **and** 8 (5 mm) **or** sizes
   needed for gauge
Markers
Yarn needle

GAUGE: With larger size needles,
in pattern (8 rows Stockinette Stitch
and 2 rows K1, P1 ribbing),
17 sts = 4" (10 cm)
30 rows = 5" (12.5 cm)
Row gauge as well as stitch gauge is very important in raglans. Be sure to make a gauge swatch.

Sweater is worked from the neck down, in one piece to underarm.

RAGLAN SHAPING
NECK RIBBING
With smaller size 16" (40.5 cm) circular needle, cast on {60-60}{68-72-76} sts **loosely** *(see Circular Knitting, page 43)*; place marker to mark beginning of rnd *(see Markers, page 43)*.

Rnds 1-6 (Right side)**:** (K1, P1) around.

YOKE
Change to larger size 16" (40.5 cm) circular needle.

Tip: Use a different color marker to indicate the increase placement.

Rnd 1: K {19-19}{21-23-25} (for Front), place marker, K1, place marker, K {9-9}{11-11-11} (for Sleeve), place marker, K1, place marker, K {19-19}{21-23-25} (for Back), place marker, K1, place marker, K {9-9}{11-11-11} (for Sleeve), place marker, K1.

Instructions continued on page 26.

Barbie had met Ellen at the bookstore the day before, when she'd come in to buy a couple of romances. The child was sweet and unpretentious; she obviously idolized Anne Marie and was completely in love with her dog, Baxter. She'd watched with some amusement as Ellen struggled to teach the Yorkie to roll over, with no success.

—Barbie

Rnd 2 (Increase rnd): ★ Slip marker, M1 *(Figs. 10a & b, page 44)*, knit across to next marker, M1, slip marker, K1; repeat from ★ around: {68-68}{76-80-84} sts.

Rnd 3: Knit around.

Rnds 4-8: Repeat Rnds 2 and 3 twice, then repeat Rnd 2 once **more**: {92-92}{100-104-108} sts.

Rnd 9: (P1, K1) around.

Rnd 10 (Increase rnd): ★ Slip marker, M1, work in established ribbing across to next marker, M1, slip marker, K1; repeat from ★ around: {100-100}{108-112-116} sts.

Change to longer circular needle when stitches become crowded on needle.

Maintaining established pattern (knit 8 rounds, work 2 ribbing rounds), continue to increase one stitch on **each** side of Back and Front, every other round, {6-9}{8-9-10} times, then increase every fourth round, {2-1}{3-3-3} time(s) **more** AND AT THE SAME TIME increase one stitch on **each** side of Sleeves, every other round, {2-3}{0-1-2} time(s) *(see Zeros, page 43)*, then increase every fourth round, {4-4}{7-7-7} times **more**: {45-49}{53-57-61} sts on Front and Back; {31-33}{35-37-39} sts on each Sleeve; a total of {156-168}{180-192-204} sts.

Tip: At this point, if you want to try the sweater on your child to check fit, the stitches can be temporarily placed on scrap yarn enabling you to do so.

LEFT SLEEVE

Note: The K1's are part of the Front and Back.

Row 1 (Dividing row): Remove marker, work in pattern across Front to next marker, remove marker, K1, remove marker; with larger size straight needles, work in pattern across Sleeve to next marker, remove marker.

Work in rows on Sleeve only, maintaining Stockinette Stitch (knit right side rows and purl wrong side rows) and ribbing pattern. Leave remaining stitches on circular needle to be worked later.

Rows 2 and 3: Add on 4 sts *(Figs. 7a & b, page 44)*, work across: {39-41}{43-45-47} sts.

Work even for {12-12}{12-20-20} rows.

Decrease Row: [Slip 1 as if to **knit**, K1, PSSO *(Figs. 13a & b, page 45)*], work across to last 2 sts, K2 tog *(Fig. 11, page 44)*: {37-39}{41-43-45} sts.

Continue to decrease one stitch at **each** edge, every sixth row, {2-6}{8-8-9} times; then decrease every fourth row, {5-1}{0-0-0} time(s) **more**: {23-25}{25-27-27} sts.

Work even until Sleeve measures approximately {8½-9¾}{11-12½-13½}"/{21.5-25}{28-32-34.5} cm from underarm, ending by working a **purl** row.

Change to smaller size needles.

Row 1: K1, (P1, K1) across.

Work in established ribbing for 2" (5 cm).

Bind off all sts **loosely** in ribbing, leaving a long end for sewing.

RIGHT SLEEVE

Row 1 (Dividing row)**:** K1, remove marker, work in pattern across Back to next marker, remove marker, K1, remove marker; with larger size straight needles, work in pattern across Sleeve to next marker, remove marker.

Work same as Left Sleeve.

Weave Sleeve seams *(Fig. 21, page 46)*.

BODY

Rnd 1: With **right** side facing and beginning at center of right underarm, pick up 2 sts in added on sts, work across Front, pick up 5 sts in added on sts, work across Back, pick up 3 sts in added on sts, place marker to mark beginning of rnd: {104-112}{120-128-136} sts.

Work in rounds maintaining pattern until Body measures approximately {7-8}{9-9¹/₂-10}"/ {18-20.5}{23-24-25.5} cm from underarm **or** 2" (5 cm) less than desired length.

Change to smaller size needles.

Work in K1, P1 ribbing for 2" (5 cm).

Bind off all sts in ribbing.

Design by Jeannine C. Laroche.

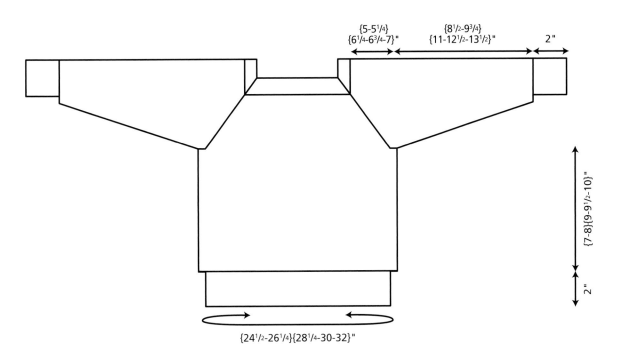

{5-5¹/₄}
{6¹/₄-6³/₄-7}"

{8¹/₂-9³/₄}
{11-12¹/₂-13¹/₂}"

2"

{7-8}{9-9¹/₂-10}"

2"

{24¹/₂-26¹/₄}{28¹/₄-30-32}"

parisian dream beret set

*Robert had promised to take Anne Marie to Paris. And he hadn't.
But she had read enough about goal-setting to realize the value of
writing things down. Already she felt a tiny bit of hope that one
day she would wear a jaunty beret and tour the famous City of Light.*

Flower Scarf: ◖■■□□ EASY
Beret: ◖■■■□ INTERMEDIATE

MATERIALS
Medium Weight Yarn
[1.5 ounces, 84 yards
(40 grams, 71 meters) per skein]:
   Camel - 7 skeins
   Black - 1 skein (for embroidery)
   Cream - 1 skein (for embroidery)
Scarf:
Straight knitting needles, size 8 (5 mm)
   or size needed for gauge
Beret:
Set of 5 double pointed needles,
   size 8 (5 mm) **or** size needed for gauge
16" (40.5 cm) Circular knitting needles,
   sizes 7 (4.5 mm) **and** 8 (5 mm) **or** sizes
needed for gauge
Yarn needle

SCARF
Finished Size: 4" x 48" (10 cm x 122 cm)

GAUGE: 11 bamboo sts (22 sts) and
            20 rows = 4" (10 cm)

With Camel and straight needles, cast on 22 sts.

Row 1: Purl across.

Row 2: ★ YO, K2, pass YO over 2 knit sts; repeat
from ★ across *(Fig. 6a, page 43)*.

Repeat Rows 1 and 2 for bamboo stitch until
Scarf measures approximately 48" (122 cm) from
cast on edge **or** to desired length, ending by
working Row 1.

Bind off all stitches in **knit**.

EMBROIDERY
Using the placement diagram as a guide,
embroider 6 flowers on Scarf, working Black
stem stitch vines and Cream lazy daisy leaves
with bullion knot flowers *(see Embroidery
Stitches, page 47)* and placing 3 flowers evenly
spaced across half of scarf and 3 across second
half of Scarf, facing in opposite direction.

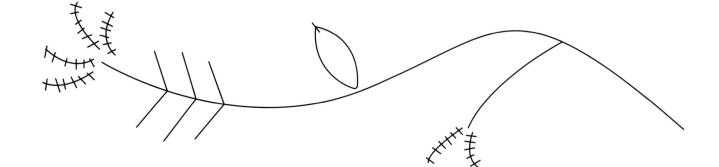

28

Beret instructions begin on page 30.

"The wishes don't need to be practical," Anne Marie went on to explain to Ellen. "That's why they're called wishes instead of resolutions or goals."

Reaching for a pen, she added a wish she'd erased two or three times.

10. Travel to Paris with someone I love.

That encompassed the essence of what she sought—love, adventure, new experiences.

—Anne Marie

BERET
INNER CAP
GAUGE: With larger size needles,
In Stockinette Stitch,
17 sts and 25 rnds = 4" (10 cm)

With double pointed needles *(see Double Pointed Needles, page 43)*, using Camel and leaving a long end, cast on 8 sts and divide evenly on 4 needles.

Rnds 1 and 2 (Right side)**:** Knit around.

Rnd 3: (K1, M1) around *(Figs. 10a & b, page 44)*: 16 sts.

Rnd 4 AND ALL EVEN NUMBERED RNDS: Knit around.

Rnd 5: (K2, M1) around: 24 sts.

Rnd 7: (K3, M1) around: 32 sts.

Rnd 9: (K4, M1) around: 40 sts.

Rnd 11: (K5, M1) around: 48 sts.

Rnd 13: (K6, M1) around: 56 sts.

Rnd 15: (K7, M1) around: 64 sts.

Rnd 17: Knit around.

Rnd 19: (K8, M1) around: 72 sts.

Change to larger size circular needle, placing marker to indicate beginning of rounds.

Knit each round until piece measures approximately 7" (18 cm) from center.

Cut yarn, slip sts on smaller size circular needle to be finished later.

Using long end, close hole at center of Inner Cap.

TOP
GAUGE: With larger size needles,
Rnds 1-10 = 3" (7.5 cm) diameter
12 bamboo sts (24 sts) and
20 rnds = 3" (7.5 cm)

With double pointed needles, using Camel and leaving a long end, cast on 6 sts onto one needle.

Foundation Row (Right side)**:** Knit in front and back of each st across; divide sts evenly on 3 needles: 12 sts.

Rnd 1: Knit in front and back of each st around: 24 sts.

To work bamboo st, YO *(Fig. 6a, page 43)*, K2, pass YO over 2 knit sts.

Rnd 2: Work bamboo st around.

When working M1 over a bamboo st, insert left needle under strand formed by YO.

Rnd 3: (M1, K2) around: 36 sts.

Rnd 4: (K1, work bamboo st) around.

Rnd 5: (M1, K3) around: 48 sts.

Rnd 6: Work bamboo st around.

Rnd 7: (M1, K4) around: 60 sts.

Rnd 8: (K1, work 2 bamboo sts) around.

Rnd 9: (M1, K5) around: 72 sts.

Change to larger size circular needle.

Rnd 10: Work bamboo st around.

Rnd 11: (M1, K6) around: 84 sts.

Rnd 12: (K1, work 3 bamboo sts) around.

Rnd 13: (M1, K7) around: 96 sts.

Rnd 14: Work bamboo st around.

Rnd 15: (M1, K8) around: 108 sts.

Rnd 16: (K1, work 4 bamboo sts) around.

Rnd 17: (M1, K9) around: 120 sts.

Rnd 18: Work bamboo st around.

Rnd 19: (M1, K 10) around: 132 sts.

Rnd 20: (K1, work 5 bamboo sts) around.

Rnd 21: (M1, K 11) around: 144 sts.

Rnd 22: Work bamboo st around.

Rnd 23: (M1, K 12) around: 156 sts.

Rnd 24: (K1, work 6 bamboo sts) around.

Rnd 25: (M1, K 13) around: 168 sts.

Rnd 26: Work bamboo st around.

Rnd 27: (M1, K 14) around: 180 sts.

Rnd 28: (K1, work 7 bamboo sts) around.

Rnd 29: (M1, K 15) around: 192 sts.

Rnd 30: Work bamboo st around.

Rnd 31: (M1, K 16) around: 204 sts.

Rnd 32: (K1, work 8 bamboo sts) around.

Rnd 33: (M1, K 17) around: 216 sts.

Rnd 34: Work bamboo st around.

SIDE
Rnd 1 (Turning ridge)**:** Purl around.

Rnd 2: Knit around.

Rnd 3: Work bamboo st around.

Rnd 4: (K2 tog, K 16) around (*Fig. 11, page 44*): 204 sts.

Rnd 5: (K1, work 8 bamboo sts) around.

Rnd 6: (K2 tog, K 15) around: 192 sts.

Rnd 7: Work bamboo st around.

Rnd 8: (K2 tog, K 14) around: 180 sts.

Rnd 9: (K1, work 7 bamboo sts) around.

Rnd 10: (K2 tog, K 13) around: 168 sts.

Rnd 11: Work bamboo st around.

Rnd 12: (K2 tog, K 12) around: 156 sts.

Rnd 13: (K1, work 6 bamboo sts) around.

Rnd 14: (K2 tog, K 11) around: 144 sts.

RIBBING
Note: You may use a separate smaller size circular needle to work the first round if it will be easier for you.

With **wrong** sides together, place Inner Cap inside Top, holding needles parallel. Using smaller size circular needle, ★ insert needle in 2 sts on front needle **and** in 1 st on back needle and knit all 3 sts together; repeat from ★ around: 72 sts.

Work in K1, P1 ribbing for 1½" (4 cm).

Bind off all sts in ribbing.

Using long end, close hole at center of Top.

Design by Cathy Hardy.

keepsake doily

Celebrations are times for using your prettiest home accessories. To help Anne Marie decorate for Melissa's reception, Lydia shared one of her finest keepsakes, a doily knit of cotton thread. It starts with a crochet-hook cast-on and ends with a dainty chain link edging.

■■■□ INTERMEDIATE

Finished Size: 13" (33 cm) diameter

MATERIALS
Bedspread Weight Cotton Thread (size 10) [1,000 yards (914 meters) per ball]:
  1 ball
4 Double pointed knitting needles, size 1
  (2.25 mm) **or** size needed for gauge
Steel crochet hook, size 4 (2 mm)
Rust proof straight pins or T pins
Blocking board
Spray starch or fabric stiffener

GAUGE: In Stockinette Stitch,
     18 sts and 24 rows = 2" (5 cm)

Gauge Swatch: 3½" (9 cm) diameter
Work same as Doily through Rnd 19.

DOILY
Make a beginning loop as follows: Wrap the thread clockwise around your left index finger twice. Insert the crochet hook under both strands, yarn over (by bringing the thread over the top of the hook from back to front) *(Fig. 1a)* and pull thread through loop, yarn over and pull thread through the stitch on the hook **(counts as first cast on stitch)**; remove finger from loop.

For next cast on stitch: yarn over, insert hook in loop, yarn over and pull thread through loop, yarn over and draw through 2 loops on hook *(Fig. 1b)*.

Fig. 1a   Fig. 1b

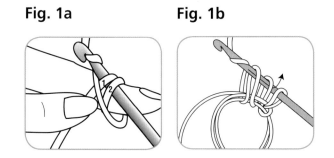

Crochet cast on a total of 6 sts and transfer 2 sts to each of 3 needles *(see Double Pointed Needles, page 43)*.

Rnd 1 (Right side): (K1, YO) across each needle *(Fig. 6a, page 43)*: 4 sts each needle; 12 sts total.

Rnds 2-4: Knit around.

Rnd 5: (K1, YO) across each needle: 8 sts each needle; 24 sts total.

Rnds 6-8: Knit around.

Rnd 9: (K1, YO twice) across each needle: 24 sts each needle; 72 sts total.

Instructions continued on page 34.

All the retailers on Blossom Street were friends. Hearing about the small party, Lydia had insisted that Anne Marie dress up her work table with a lovely cotton-knit cloth. It was so beautiful it reawakened Anne Marie's desire to learn to knit.

—Anne Marie

Rnd 10: (K2, P1) across each needle.

Rnds 11 and 12: Knit around.

When instructed to slip a stitch that will be used in a decrease, always slip as if to **knit**.

Rnd 13: ★ K3, [slip 1, K1, PSSO *(Figs. 13a & b, page 45)*], K3, YO; repeat from ★ across each needle.

Rnd 14 AND ALL EVEN NUMBERED RNDS: Knit around.

Rnd 15: ★ K2, [slip 1, K2 tog, PSSO *(Fig. 15, page 45)*], K2, YO, K1, YO; repeat from ★ across each needle.

Rnd 17: ★ K1, slip 1, K2 tog, PSSO, K1, YO, K3, YO; repeat from ★ across each needle.

Rnd 19: ★ Slip 1, K2 tog, PSSO, YO, K2 tog, YO, K1, YO, slip 1, K1, PSSO, YO; repeat from ★ across each needle.

Rnd 21: (K1, YO) across each needle: 48 sts each needle; 144 sts total.

Rnd 23: ★ YO, K1, YO, K6, slip 1, K2 tog, PSSO, K6; repeat from ★ across each needle.

Rnd 25: ★ YO, K3, YO, K5, slip 1, K2 tog, PSSO, K5; repeat from ★ across each needle.

Rnd 27: ★ YO, K2 tog, YO, K1, YO, slip 1, K1, PSSO, YO, K4, slip 1, K2 tog, PSSO, K4; repeat from ★ across each needle.

Rnd 29: ★ YO, K2 tog, YO, K3, YO, slip 1, K1, PSSO, YO, K3, slip 1, K2 tog, PSSO, K3; repeat from ★ across each needle.

Rnd 31: ★ (YO, K2 tog) twice, YO, K1, YO, (slip 1, K1, PSSO, YO) twice, K2, slip 1, K2 tog, PSSO, K2; repeat from ★ across each needle.

Rnd 33: ★ (YO, K2 tog) twice, YO, K3, YO, (slip 1, K1, PSSO, YO) twice, K1, slip 1, K2 tog, PSSO, K1; repeat from ★ across each needle.

Rnd 35: ★ (YO, K2 tog) 3 times, YO, K1, YO, (slip 1, K1, PSSO, YO) 3 times, slip 1, K2 tog, PSSO; repeat from ★ across each needle.

Rnd 37: (K1, YO) across each needle: 96 sts each needle; 288 sts total.

Rnd 39: ★ K 13, slip 1, K2 tog, PSSO, K 13, YO, K3, YO; repeat from ★ across each needle.

Rnd 41: ★ K 12, slip 1, K2 tog, PSSO, K 12, YO, K5, YO; repeat from ★ across each needle.

Rnd 43: ★ K 11, slip 1, K2 tog, PSSO, K 11, YO, K7, YO; repeat from ★ across each needle.

Rnd 45: ★ K 10, slip 1, K2 tog, PSSO, K 10, YO, K9, YO; repeat from ★ across each needle.

Rnd 47: ★ K9, slip 1, K2 tog, PSSO, K9, YO, K 11, YO; repeat from ★ across each needle.

Rnd 49: ★ K8, slip 1, K2 tog, PSSO, K8, YO, K 13, YO; repeat from ★ across each needle.

Rnd 51: ★ K7, slip 1, K2 tog, PSSO, K7, YO, K 15, YO; repeat from ★ across each needle.

Rnd 53: ★ K6, slip 1, K2 tog, PSSO, K6, YO, K 17, YO; repeat from ★ across each needle.

Rnd 55: ★ K5, slip 1, K2 tog, PSSO, K5, YO, K 19, YO; repeat from ★ across each needle.

Rnd 57: ★ K4, slip 1, K2 tog, PSSO, K4, YO, K 21, YO; repeat from ★ across each needle.

Rnd 59: ★ K3, slip 1, K2 tog, PSSO, K3, YO, K 23, YO; repeat from ★ across each needle.

Rnd 61: ★ K2, slip 1, K2 tog, PSSO, K2, YO, K 25, YO; repeat from ★ across each needle.

Rnd 63: ★ K1, slip 1, K2 tog, PSSO, K1, YO, K 27, YO; repeat from ★ across each needle.

Rnd 65: ★ Slip 1, K2 tog, PSSO, YO, K 29, YO; repeat from ★ across each needle.

To make a chain: Yarn over and draw the thread through the stitch on the hook *(Fig. 2a)*; repeat for each chain required.

Fig. 2a

To work off sts: Insert hook through 3 sts on left needle *(Fig. 2b)* and slip them off the needle, YO and draw through all loops on hook.

Fig. 2b

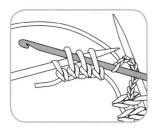

Rnd 67: Slip 1 st from the right needle to the left needle, insert crochet hook in last st on right needle *(Fig. 3)*, ★ (chain 10, work off 3 sts) 5 times, chain 10, work off 5 sts, (chain 10, work off 3 sts) 4 times; repeat from ★ across each needle; insert hook in first chain of beginning chain 10, YO and draw through st and loop on hook.

Fig. 3

Wash and block Doily *(see Washing and Blocking, page 47)*.

Spray **wrong** side of Doily lightly with starch or fabric stiffener. Spread Doily on blocking board and stretch to shape; pin chain loops in place until dry.

Design by Larisa Scott.

35

positively pretty pullover

Cheered by the color of Lillie's new BMW convertible, Anne Marie selected a rich red yarn for the pullover she wanted to knit for herself. She was ready to take on more challenging projects now that she had some experience, and she found the eyelet border patterns appealing.

◼◼◼◻ INTERMEDIATE

Size	Finished Bust Measurement	
X-Small	32½"	(82.5 cm)
Small	35½"	(90 cm)
Medium	39"	(99 cm)
Large	45"	(114.5 cm)
X-Large	48½"	(123 cm)

Note: Instructions are written for sizes X-Small and Small in the first set of braces { }, with sizes Medium, Large and X-Large in the second set of braces. Instructions will be easier to read if you circle all the numbers pertaining to your size. If only one number is given, it applies to all sizes.

MATERIALS

Medium Weight Yarn
[2.8 ounces, 145 yards
(80 grams, 133 meters) per skein]:
  {7-8}{9-10-11} skeins
Straight knitting needles, size 7 (4.5 mm)
  or size needed for gauge
16" (40.5 cm) Circular knitting needle,
  size 5 (3.75 mm)
Stitch holders - 2
Yarn needle

GAUGE: With larger size needles,
  in Stockinette Stitch,
  20 sts and 26 rows = 4" (10 cm)

BACK
BORDER
With straight needles, cast on {83-91}{99-115-123} sts.

Row 1: P1, (K1, P1) across.

Row 2: K1, (P1, K1) across.

Row 3: P1, (K1, P1) across.

Row 4 (Right side): K3, K2 tog *(Fig. 11, page 44)*, YO *(Fig. 6a, page 43)*, K1, YO, [slip 1 as if to **knit**, K1, PSSO *(Figs. 13a & b, page 45)*], K3, ★ K2 tog, YO, K1, YO, slip 1 as if to **knit**, K1, PSSO, K3; repeat from ★ across.

Row 5 AND ALL WRONG SIDE ROWS: Purl across.

Row 6: K2, K2 tog, YO, K3, YO, slip 1 as if to **knit**, K1, PSSO, ★ K1, K2 tog, YO, K3, YO, slip 1 as if to **knit**, K1, PSSO; repeat from ★ across to last 2 sts, K2.

Row 8: K1, K2 tog, YO, K5, ★ YO, [slip 1 as if to **knit**, K2 tog, PSSO *(Fig. 15, page 45)*], YO, K5; repeat from ★ across to last 3 sts, YO, slip 1 as if to **knit**, K1, PSSO, K1.

Row 10: K1, slip 1 as if to **knit**, K1, PSSO, YO, K5, ★ YO, [slip 2 tog as if to **knit**, K1, P2SSO *(Fig. 16, page 45)*], YO, K5; repeat from ★ across to last 3 sts, YO, K2 tog, K1.

Whenever Anne Marie went into the yarn shop, she was astonished by the range of beautiful colors and inviting textures. Putting down her packages, she reached out one hand to touch a skein of irresistibly soft wool.

—Anne Marie

Row 12: K1, slip 1 as if to **knit**, K1, PSSO, YO, K5, ★ YO, slip 2 tog as if to **knit**, K1, P2SSO, YO, K5; repeat from ★ across to last 3 sts, YO, K2 tog, K1.

Row 14: K3, ★ YO, slip 1 as if to **knit**, K1, PSSO, K1, K2 tog, YO, K3; repeat from ★ across.

Row 16: K4, YO, slip 1 as if to **knit**, K2 tog, PSSO, YO, ★ K5, YO, slip 1 as if to **knit**, K2 tog, PSSO, YO; repeat from ★ across to last 4 sts, K4.

BODY
Beginning with a purl row, work in Stockinette Stitch (purl one row, knit one row) until piece measures approximately {15-15}{15-16-16}"/ {38-38}{38-40.5-40.5} cm from cast on edge, ending by working a **purl** row.

Instructions continued on page 38.

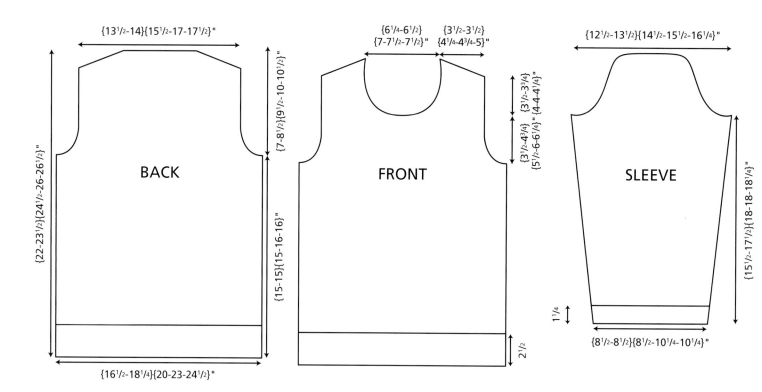

The schematic diagrams show measurements:

BACK: {13½-14}{15½-17-17½}" (top), {7-8½}{9½-10-10½}" (right upper), {15-15}{15-16-16}" (right lower), {22-23½}{24½-26-26½}" (left side), {16½-18¼}{20-23-24½}" (bottom)

FRONT: {6¼-6½}{7-7½-7½}" and {3½-3½}{4¼-4¾-5}" (top), {3½-3¾}{4-4-4¼}" and {3½-4¾}{5½-6-6¼}" (right), 2½ (bottom right)

SLEEVE: {12½-13½}{14½-15½-16¼}" (top), {15½-17½}{18-18-18¼}" (right side), 1¼ (left), {8½-8½}{8½-10¼-10¼}" (bottom)

ARMHOLE SHAPING
Rows 1 and 2: Bind off {5-6}{6-8-10} sts, work across: {73-79}{87-99-103} sts.

Row 3 (Decrease row): Slip 1 as if to **knit**, K1, PSSO, knit across to last 2 sts, K2 tog: {71-77}{85-97-101} sts.

Row 4: Purl across.

Repeat Rows 3 and 4, {2-4}{4-6-7} times: {67-69}{77-85-87} sts.

Work even until Armholes measure approximately {7-8½}{9½-10-10½}"/ {18-21.5}{24-25.5-26.5} cm, ending by working a **purl** row.

SHOULDER SHAPING
Rows 1-4: Bind off {6-6}{7-8-8} sts, work across: {43-45}{49-53-55} sts.

Rows 5 and 6: Bind off {6-6}{7-8-9} sts, work across: {31-33}{35-37-37} sts.

Slip remaining sts onto st holder; cut yarn.

FRONT
Work same as Back until Armholes measure approximately {3½-4¾}{5½-6-6¼}"/{9-12}{14-15-16} cm, ending by working a **knit** row: {67-69}{77-85-87} sts.

NECK SHAPING
Both sides of the Neck are worked at the same time, using separate yarn for **each** side.

Row 1: Purl {24-24}{27-30-31} sts, slip next {19-21}{23-25-25} sts onto st holder; with second yarn, purl across: {24-24}{27-30-31} sts **each** side.

Row 2 (Decrease row): Knit across to within 2 sts of neck edge, K2 tog; with second yarn, slip 1 as if to **knit**, K1, PSSO, knit across: {23-23}{26-29-30} sts **each** side.

Row 3 (Decrease row): Purl across to within 2 sts of neck edge, P2 tog tbl *(Fig. 18, page 46)*; with second yarn, P2 tog *(Fig. 17, page 45)*, purl across: {22-22}{25-28-29} sts **each** side.

Row 4 (Decrease row): Knit across to within 2 sts of neck edge, K2 tog; with second yarn, slip 1 as if to **knit**, K1, PSSO, knit across: {21-21}{24-27-28} sts **each** side.

Row 5: Purl across; with second yarn, purl across.

Rows 6-11: Repeat Rows 4 and 5, 3 times: {18-18}{21-24-25} sts **each** side.

Work even until Front measures same as Back to Shoulder Shaping, ending by working a **purl** row.

SHOULDER SHAPING

Rows 1-4: Bind off {6-6}{7-8-8} sts, work across; with second yarn, work across: {6-6}{7-8-9} sts **each** side.

Row 5: Bind off remaining sts on first side; with second yarn, work across.

Bind off remaining sts.

SLEEVE (Make 2)
BORDER

With straight needles, cast on {43-43}{43-51-51} sts.

Row 1: P1, (K1, P1) across.

Row 2: K1, (P1, K1) across.

Row 3: P1, (K1, P1) across.

Row 4 (Right side): K3, ★ K2 tog, YO, K1, YO, slip 1 as if to **knit**, K1, PSSO, K3; repeat from ★ across.

Row 5: Purl across.

Row 6: K2, K2 tog, YO, K3, YO, slip 1 as if to **knit**, K1, PSSO, ★ K1, K2 tog, YO, K3, YO, slip 1 as if to **knit**, K1, PSSO; repeat from ★ across to last 2 sts, K2.

Row 7: Purl across.

Row 8: K1, K2 tog, YO, K5, ★ YO, slip 1 as if to **knit**, K2 tog, PSSO, YO, K5; repeat from ★ across to last 3 sts, YO, slip 1 as if to **knit**, K1, PSSO, K1.

BODY

Beginning with a purl row, work in Stockinette Stitch, increasing one stitch at **each** edge *(Figs. 9a & b, page 44)*, every sixth row, {4-5}{15-8-15} times; then increase every eighth row, {6-7}{0-5-0} times **more** *(see Zeros, page 43)*: {63-67}{73-77-81} sts.

Work even until Sleeve measures approximately {15$\frac{1}{2}$-17$\frac{1}{2}$}{18-18-18$\frac{1}{4}$}"/ {39.5-44.5}{45.5-45.5-46.5} cm from cast on edge, ending by working a **purl** row.

SLEEVE CAP

Rows 1 and 2: Bind off {5-6}{6-8-10} sts, work across: {53-55}{61-61-61} sts.

Row 3 (Decrease row): Slip 1 as if to **knit**, K1, PSSO, knit across to last 2 sts, K2 tog: {51-53}{59-59-59} sts.

Continue to decrease one stitch at **each** edge, every other row, {6-4}{5-2-1} time(s); then decrease every fourth row, {2-5}{7-9-10} times **more**: {35-35}{35-37-37} sts.

Bind off 4 sts at the beginning of the next 6 rows, work across: {11-11}{11-13-13} sts.

Bind off remaining sts.

FINISHING

Sew shoulder seams.

NECK RIBBING

With **right** side facing and using circular needle, pick up and knit {26-28}{30-30-32} sts evenly spaced along left Front Neck edge *(Fig. 19, page 46)*, knit {19-21}{23-25-25} sts from Front st holder, pick up and knit {26-28}{30-30-32} sts evenly spaced along right Front Neck edge, slip {31-33}{35-37-37} sts from Back st holder onto empty point and knit across; place marker to indicate beginning of round *(see Markers, page 43)*: {102-110}{118-122-126} sts.

Work in K1, P1 ribbing for 3 rounds.

Bind off all sts **loosely** in ribbing.

Sew Sleeves to pullover, placing center of Sleeve Cap at shoulder seam and matching bound off stitches.

Weave underarm and side in one continuous seam *(Fig. 21, page 46)*.

Design by Cathy Hardy.

thank you for helping warm up america!

Since 1991, Warm Up America! has donated more than 250,000 afghans to battered women's shelters, victims of natural disaster, the homeless, and many others who are in need.

You can help Warm Up America! help others, and with so little effort. Debbie urges everyone who uses the patterns in this book to take a few minutes to knit a 7" x 9" block for this worthy cause. To help you get started, she's providing this block pattern.

If you are able to provide a completed afghan, Warm Up America requests that you donate it directly to any charity or social services agency in your community. If you require assistance in assembling the blocks into an afghan, please include your name and address inside the packaging and ship your 7" x 9" blocks to:

Warm Up America! Foundation
2500 Lowell Road
Ranlo, NC 28054

Remember, just a little bit of yarn can make a big difference to someone in need!

Basic patchwork afghans are made of forty-nine 7" x 9" (18 cm x 23 cm) rectangular blocks that are sewn together. Any pattern stitch can be used for the rectangle. Use acrylic medium weight yarn and size 8 (5 mm) straight knitting needles or size needed to obtain the gauge of 9 stitches to 2" (5 cm).

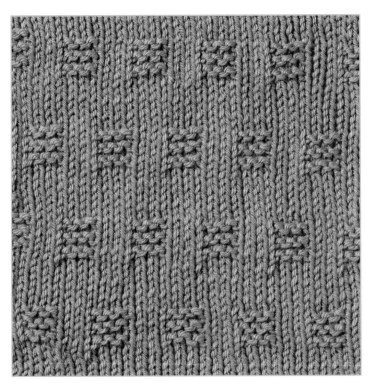

CHECKS BLOCK

Multiple of 6 sts + 3.

Cast on 33 sts.

Row 1: Purl across.

Row 2 (Right side)**:** Knit across.

Rows 3-6: Repeat Rows 1 and 2 twice.

Row 7: Purl across.

Row 8: K3, (P3, K3) across.

Rows 9-12: Repeat Rows 7 and 8 twice.

Rows 13-18: Repeat Rows 1 and 2, 3 times.

Row 19: Purl across.

Row 20: P3, (K3, P3) across.

Rows 21-24: Repeat Rows 19 and 20 twice.

Repeat Rows 1-24 for pattern until Block measures approximately 9" (23 cm) from cast on edge, ending by working Row 6 or Row 18.

Bind off all sts in **purl**.

general instructions

ABBREVIATIONS

cm	centimeters
K	knit
M1	make one
mm	millimeters
P	purl
PSSO	pass slipped stitch(es) over
P2SSO	pass 2 slipped stitch(es) over
Rnd(s)	round(s)
st(s)	stitch(es)
tbl	through back loop
tog	together
YO	yarn over

★ — work instructions following ★ as many **more** times as indicated in addition to the first time.

( ) or [ ] — work enclosed instructions **as many** times as specified by the number immediately following **or** work all enclosed instructions in the stitch indicated **or** contains explanatory remarks.

Colon (:) — the number given after a colon at the end of a row or round denotes the number of stitches you should have on that row or round.

Work even — work without increasing or decreasing in the established pattern.

GAUGE

Exact gauge is **essential** for proper size. Before beginning your project, make a sample swatch in the yarn and needle specified in the individual instructions. After completing the swatch, measure it, counting your stitches and rows or rounds carefully. If your swatch is larger or smaller than specified, **make another, changing needle size to get the correct gauge**. Keep trying until you find the size needles that will give you the specified gauge. Once proper gauge is obtained, measure width of project approximately every 3" (7.5 cm) to be sure gauge remains consistent.

KNIT TERMINOLOGY	
UNITED STATES	**INTERNATIONAL**
gauge =	tension
bind off =	cast off
yarn over (YO) =	yarn forward (yfwd) **or**
	yarn around needle (yrn)

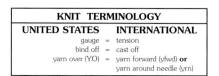

Yarn Weight Symbol & Names	SUPER FINE 1	FINE 2	LIGHT 3	MEDIUM 4	BULKY 5	SUPER BULKY 6
Type of Yarns in Category	Sock, Fingering Baby	Sport, Baby	DK, Light Worsted	Worsted, Afghan, Aran	Chunky, Craft, Rug	Bulky, Roving
Knit Gauge Ranges in Stockinette St to 4" (10 cm)	27-32 sts	23-26 sts	21-24 sts	16-20 sts	12-15 sts	6-11 sts
Advised Needle Size Range	1-3	3-5	5-7	7-9	9-11	11 and larger

◼◻◻◻ BEGINNER		Projects for first-time knitters using basic knit and purl stitches. Minimal shaping.
◼◼◻◻ EASY		Projects using basic stitches, repetitive stitch patterns, simple color changes, and simple shaping and finishing.
◼◼◼◻ INTERMEDIATE		Projects with a variety of stitches, such as basic cables and lace, simple intarsia, double-pointed needles and knitting in the round needle techniques, mid-level shaping and finishing.
◼◼◼◼ EXPERIENCED		Projects using advanced techniques and stitches, such as short rows, fair isle, more intricate intarsia, cables, lace patterns, and numerous color changes.

KNITTING NEEDLES															
U.S.	0	1	2	3	4	5	6	7	8	9	10	10½	11	13	15	17
U.K.	13	12	11	10	9	8	7	6	5	4	3	2	1	00	000	---
Metric - mm	2	2.25	2.75	3.25	3.5	3.75	4	4.5	5	5.5	6	6.5	8	9	10	12.75

MARKERS

As a convenience to you, we have used markers to mark the beginning of a round, help distinguish the beginning of a pattern, or to mark placement of increases. Place markers as instructed. You may use purchased markers or tie a length of contrasting color yarn around the needle. When you reach a marker on each row or round, slip it from the left needle to the right needle; remove it when no longer needed.

CIRCULAR KNITTING

When you knit in rounds, you are going to work around on the outside of the circle, with the **right** side of the knitting facing you.

Cast on the number of stitches indicated. Make sure the cast on ridge lays on the inside of the needle and never rolls around the needle *(Fig.4)*. Hold the needle so that the ball of yarn is attached to the stitch closest to the right hand point. Place a marker on the right hand point to mark the beginning of the rounds *(see Markers)*. Knit the stitches on the left hand point.

Fig. 4

DOUBLE POINTED NEEDLES

The stitches are divided evenly between three or four double pointed needles as specified in the individual pattern, depending on the number of petals or patterns in the Doily or Beret. Form a triangle with the three needles, or a square with the four needles. Do **not** twist the cast on ridge. With the remaining needle, work across the stitches on the first needle *(Fig. 5)*. You will now have an empty needle with which to knit the stitches from the next needle. Work the first stitch of each needle firmly to prevent gaps. Continue working around without turning the work. If there is a yarn over at the end of the needle, take care **not** to lose it.

Fig. 5

ZEROS

To consolidate the length of an involved pattern, Zeros are sometimes used so that all sizes can be combined. For example, increase every fourth row {3-0-5} times means that the first size would increase 3 times, the second size would do nothing, and the largest size would increase 5 times.

YARN OVERS

A yarn over *(abbreviated YO)* is simply placing the yarn over the right needle creating an extra stitch. Since the Yarn Over does produce a hole in the knit fabric, it is used for a lacy effect. On the row following a Yarn Over, you must be careful to keep it on the needle and treat it as a stitch by knitting or purling it as instructed.

To make a yarn over, you'll loop the yarn over the needle like you would to knit or purl a stitch, bringing it either to the front or the back of the piece so that it'll be ready to work the next stitch, creating a new stitch on the needle as follows:

After a knit stitch, before a knit stitch
Bring the yarn forward **between** the needles, then back **over** the top of the right hand needle, so that it is now in position to knit the next stitch *(Fig. 6a)*.

Fig. 6a

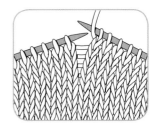

After a purl stitch, before a purl stitch

Take the yarn **over** the right hand needle to the back, then forward **between** the needles again, so that it is now in position to purl the next stitch **(Fig. 6b)**.

Fig. 6b

ADDING STITCHES

Insert the right needle into the stitch as if to **knit**, yarn over and pull loop through **(Fig. 7a)**, insert left needle into loop just worked from front to back and slip it onto the left needle **(Fig. 7b)**. Repeat for required number of stitches.

Fig. 7a

Fig. 7b

THROUGH BACK LOOP
(abbreviated tbl)

When instructed to knit or purl into the back loop of a stitch **(Fig. 8)**, the result will be twisted stitches.

Fig. 8

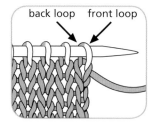

KNIT INCREASE

Knit the next stitch but do **not** slip the old stitch off the left needle **(Fig. 9a)**. Insert the right needle into the **back** loop of the **same** stitch and knit it **(Fig. 9b)**, then slip the old stitch off the left needle.

Fig. 9a

Fig.9b

MAKE ONE
(abbreviated M1)

Insert the **left** needle under the horizontal strand between the stitches from the **front (Fig. 10a)**. Then, knit into the **back** of the strand **(Fig. 10b)**.

Fig. 10a

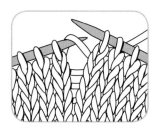

Fig. 10b

KNIT 2 TOGETHER
(abbreviated K2 tog)

Insert the right needle into the **front** of the first two stitches on the left needle as if to **knit (Fig. 11)**, then **knit** them together as if they were one stitch.

Fig. 11

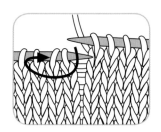

KNIT 2 TOGETHER THROUGH BACK LOOP
(abbreviated K2 tog tbl)
Insert the right needle into the **back** of the first two stitches on the left needle as if to **knit** *(Fig. 12)*, then **knit** them together as if they were one stitch.

Fig. 12

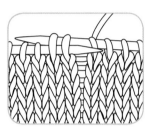

SLIP 1, KNIT 1, PASS SLIPPED STITCH OVER
(abbreviated slip 1, K1, PSSO)
Slip one stitch as if to **knit** *(Fig. 13a)*. Knit the next stitch. With the left needle, bring the slipped stitch over the knit stitch *(Fig. 13b)* and off the needle.

Fig. 13a

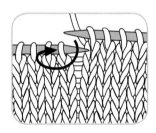

Fig. 13b

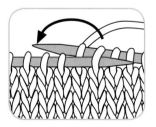

SLIP 1, KNIT 2, PASS SLIPPED STITCH OVER
(abbreviated slip 1, K2, PSSO)
Slip one stitch as if to **purl**. Knit the next two stitches. With the left needle, bring the slipped stitch over the two knit stitches *(Fig. 14)* and off the needle.

Fig. 14

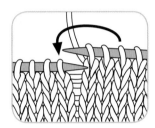

SLIP 1, KNIT 2 TOGETHER, PASS SLIPPED STITCH OVER
(abbreviated slip 1, K2 tog, PSSO)
Slip one stitch as if to **knit** *(Fig. 13a)*, then knit the next two stitches together *(Fig. 11, page 44)*. With the left needle, bring the slipped stitch over the stitch just made *(Fig. 15)* and off the needle.

Fig. 15

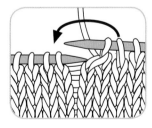

SLIP 2 TOGETHER, KNIT 1, PASS 2 SLIPPED STITCHES OVER
(abbreviated slip 2 tog, K1, P2SSO)
Slip two stitches together as if to **knit** *(Fig. 16)*, then knit the next stitch. With the left needle, bring the two slipped stitches over the stitch just made and off the needle.

Fig. 16

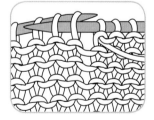

PURL 2 TOGETHER
(abbreviated P2 tog)
Insert the right needle into the **front** of the first two stitches on the left needle as if to **purl** *(Fig. 17)*, then **purl** them together as if they were one stitch.

Fig. 17

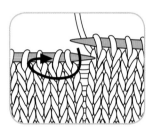

PURL 2 TOGETHER THROUGH BACK LOOP

(abbreviated P2 tog tbl)

Insert the right needle into the **back** of the first two stitches on the left needle from **back** to **front** *(Fig. 18)*, then **purl** them together as if they were one stitch.

Fig. 18

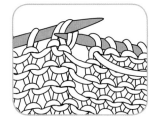

PICKING UP STITCHES

When instructed to pick up stitches, insert the needle from the **front** to the **back** under two strands at the edge of the worked piece *(Fig. 19)*. Put the yarn around the needle as if to **knit**, then bring the needle with the yarn back through the stitch to the right side, resulting in a stitch on the needle. Repeat this along the edge, picking up the required number of stitches.

A crochet hook may be helpful to pull yarn through.

When instructed to **pick up and knit stitches**, pick up a stitch and slip it onto the left needle, then knit the stitch. Continue for each stitch to be picked up.

Fig. 19

WHIPSTITCH

With **right** sides together, sew through both pieces once to secure the beginning of the seam, leaving an ample yarn end to weave in later. Insert the needle from **front** to **back** through two strands on each piece *(Fig. 20)*. Bring the needle around and insert it from **front** to **back** through the next two strands on both pieces. Repeat along the edge.

Fig. 20

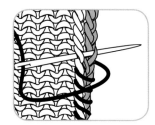

WEAVING SEAMS

With the **right** side of both pieces facing you and edges even, sew through both pieces once to secure the beginning of the seam, leaving an ample yarn end to weave in later. Insert the needle under the bar **between** the first and second stitches on the row and pull the yarn through *(Fig. 21)*. Insert the needle under the next bar on the second side. Repeat from side to side, being careful to match rows. If the edges are different lengths, it may be necessary to insert the needle under two bars at one edge.

Fig. 21

TWISTED CORD

Cut two pieces of yarn, each **3 times** as long as the desired finished length. Holding both pieces together, fasten one end to a stationary object **or** have another person hold it; twist until **tight**. Fold it in half and let it twist itself; knot both ends and cut the loops on the folded end.

TASSEL

Cut a piece of cardboard 3" (7.5 cm) square. Wind a double strand of yarn around the cardboard approximately 9 times. Cut an 18" (45.5 cm) length of yarn and insert it under all of the strands at the top of the cardboard; pull up **tightly** and tie securely. Leave the yarn ends long enough to attach the tassel. Cut the yarn at the opposite end of the cardboard *(Fig. 22a)* and then remove it. Cut a 6" (15 cm) length of yarn and wrap it **tightly** around the tassel twice, $1/2$" (1.5 cm) below the top *(Fig. 22b)*; tie securely. Trim the ends.

Fig. 22a

Fig. 22b

WASHING AND BLOCKING

For a more professional look, thread pieces should be washed and blocked. Using a mild detergent and warm water and being careful not to rub, twist, or wring, gently squeeze suds through the piece. Rinse several times in cool, clear water. Roll piece in a clean terry towel and gently press out the excess moisture. Lay piece on a flat surface and shape to proper size; where needed, pin in place using rust-proof pins. Allow to dry **completely**.

EMBROIDERY STITCHES
STEM STITCH

Bring needle up at 1, leaving an end to be woven in later. Holding yarn **above** with thumb, insert needle down at 2 and up again at 3 (halfway between 1 and 2); pull through. Insert needle down at 4 and up again at 2 *(Fig. 23)*, making sure yarn is **above** needle; pull through. Continue in this manner.

Fig. 23

LAZY DAISY STITCH

Come up at 1 and make a counterclockwise loop with the yarn. Go down at 1 and come up at 2, keeping the yarn below the point of the needle *(Fig. 24)*. Secure loop by bringing thread over loop and down at 3. Repeat for the desired number of petals or leaves. Make 1 loop for each leaf.

Fig. 24

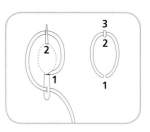

BULLION KNOT

Come up at 1. Go down at 2 leaving a loop and insert needle at 1 but don't pull it through. Using formed loop, wrap the yarn 6 times around the needle *(Fig. 25a)*. Holding wrapped stitches, pull the needle through then go down at 2 *(Fig. 25b)*. Repeat for the required number of petals.

Fig. 25a   **Fig. 25b**

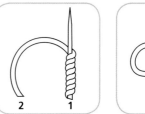

yarn information

The projects in this leaflet were made using a variety of yarns and threads. Any brand in the specified weight may be used. It is best to refer to the yardage/meters when determining how many balls or skeins to purchase. Remember, to arrive at the finished size, it is the GAUGE/TENSION that is important, not the brand of yarn.

For your convenience, listed below are the specific yarns used to create our photography models.

SEED STITCH SCARF
Bernat® Softee Chunky
#40729 Carnival

FELTED BOOK CARRIER
Patons® SWS
#70013 Natural Earth

TWO-TONE THROW
Patons® Shetland Chunky
#03022 Taupe
#03040 Black

REFRESHING SPA SET
Lion Brand® Cotton-Ease
#186 Maize

BEADED GARTER
Coats® Aunt Lydia's® Fashion
Crochet Thread
#0201P White/Pearl

BAXTER'S COZY COAT
Lion Brand® Vanna's Choice
#173 Dusty Green

PRETTY PANELS AFGHAN
Lion Brand® Jiffy®
Rose - #137 Blush
Brown - #122 Caffé

BOBBLES FOR BABY
Red Heart® Soft Yarn™
#4601 Off-White

RAGLAN RIDGE PULLOVER
Lion Brand® Cotton-Ease
#112 Berry

PARISIAN DREAM BERET SET
Lion Brand® Lion Cashmere
Blend
#124 Camel
#153 Black
#098 Cream

KEEPSAKE DOILY
Coats® Aunt Lydia's® Classic
Crochet Thread
#226 Natural

POSITIVELY PRETTY PULLOVER
Moda-Dea® Bamboo Wool™
#3920 Chili Pepper Red